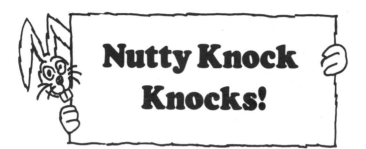

Nutty Knock Knocks!

Books by Joseph Rosenbloom

Biggest Riddle Book in the World
Daffy Definitions
Doctor Knock-Knock's Official Knock-Knock
    Dictionary
Funny Insults & Snappy Put-Downs
Gigantic Joke Book
Looniest Limerick Book in the World
Mad Scientist
Monster Madness
Official Wild West Joke Book
Polar Bears Like It Hot
Ridiculous Nicholas Haunted House Riddles
Ridiculous Nicholas Pet Riddles
Ridiculous Nicholas Riddle Book
Silly Verse (and Even Worse)
Wacky Insults and Terrible Jokes
Zaniest Riddle Book in the World

Joseph Rosenbloom
Nutty Knock Knocks!

Drawings by
Sandy Hoffman

Sterling Publishing Co., Inc. **New York**

To Brian Backerman

Library of Congress Cataloging-in-Publication Data

Rosenbloom, Joseph.
  Nutty knock knocks!
  Includes index.
  Summary: More than 500 knock-knock jokes, arranged
alphabetically.
    1. Knock-knock jokes.   2. Wit and humor, Juvenile.
[1. Knock-knock jokes.   2. Jokes]   I. Hoffman, Sandy,
ill.   II. Title.
PN6231.K55R67   1986   818'.5402   85-27626
ISBN 0-8069-6304-2 (pbk.)

Published in 1986 by Sterling Publishing Co., Inc.
387 Park Avenue South, New York, N.Y. 10016
Distributed in Canada by Sterling Publishing
% Canadian Manda Group, P.O. Box 920, Station U
Toronto, Ontario, Canada M8Z 5P9
Distributed in Great Britain and Europe by Cassell PLC
Artillery House, Artillery Row, London SW1P 1RT, England
Distributed in Australia by Capricorn Ltd.
P.O. Box 704, Windsor, NSW 2756 Australia
Printed in China

A

Knock-Knock.
  Who's there?
Aardvark.
  Aardvark who?
Aardvark-um cleaner broke. Can I borrow yours?

Knock-Knock.
  Who's there?
Abbey.
  Abbey who?
Abbey Birthday!

Knock-Knock.
  Who's there?
Achilles.
  Achilles who?
Achilles mosquitoes
with a swatter! (*Slap!*)

Knock-Knock.
  Who's there?
Ada.
  Ada who?
You're Ada your mind.

Knock-Knock.
  Who's there?
Adam.
  Adam who?
Adam my way! I'm coming in!

Knock-Knock.
  Who's there?
Addison.
  Addison who?
Addison no way to treat
an old friend.

Knock-Knock.
  Who's there?
Afghan.
  Afghan who?
Afghan away and never see you again.
    Knock-Knock.
      Who's there?
    Toodle.
      Toodle who?
    Bye-bye.

Knock-Knock.
  Who's there?
Afghanistan.
  Afghanistan who?
Afghanistan out here
all night if you
don't open the door.

Knock-Knock.
  Who's there?
Agate.
  Agate who?
Agate you covered!

Knock-Knock.
  Who's there?
Aiken.
  Aiken who?
Oh, my Aiken back!

Knock-Knock.
  Who's there?
Al and Edith.
  Al and Edith who?
"Al and Edith love . . ."

Knock-Knock.
  Who's there?
Alcott.
  Alcott who?
Alcott the cake. You pour the tea.

Knock-Knock.
    Who's there?
Alda and Alda.
    Alda and Alda who?
I'm getting Alda and Alda standing out here in the cold.

Knock-Knock.
    Who's there?
Aldo.
    Aldo who?
Aldo anything for you.

Knock-Knock.
    Who's there?
Aldous.
    Aldous who?
Aldous knocking is giving me a headache.

Knock-Knock.
Who's there?
Alex.
Alex who?
Alex-plain later. Open the door.

Knock-Knock.
Who's there?
Alfie.
Alfie who?
Alfie-give your rudeness—I know you're just being yourself.

Knock-Knock.
Who's there?
Ali.
Ali who?
Ali time you knew it was me.

Knock-Knock.
Who's there?
Aloha.
Aloha who?
Aloha, there!
Knock-Knock.
Who's there?
Hawaii.
Hawaii who?
Hawaii doing?

Knock-Knock.
Who's there?
Althea.
Althea who?
Althea in jail!

Knock-Knock.
 Who's there?
Alva and Alma.
 Alva and Alma who?
Alva day long I spend Alma time outside your door.

Knock-Knock.
 Who's there?
Alyce.
 Alyce who?
Alyce thought you were nuts.

Knock-Knock. Knock-Knock.
 Who's there?   Who's there?
Amanda Lynn. Amarillo.
 Amanda Lynn who?   Amarillo who?
Amanda Lynn player. Amarillo-ld country boy.

Knock-Knock.
 Who's there?
Amaryllis.
 Amaryllis who?
Amaryllis state agent. Want to buy a house?
  Knock-Knock.
   Who's there?
  Toboggan.
   Toboggan who?
  Yes, but I don't like toboggan.
    Knock-Knock.
     Who's there?
    Arlo.
     Arlo who?
    Arlo prices can't be beat.

Knock-Knock.
　Who's there?
Amateur.
　　Amateur who?
Amateur service.

Knock-Knock.
　Who's there?
Amen.
　Amen who?
Amen hot water again.

Knock-Knock.
　Who's there?
Amnesia.
　Amnesia who?
Oh, I see you have it, too!

Knock-Knock.
  Who's there?
Amoeba.
  Amoeba who?
"Amoeba wrong, but I think you're wonderful . . ."
    Knock-Knock.
      Who's there?
    Algae.
      Algae who?
    "Algae you in my dreams. . . ."
        Knock-Knock.
          Who's there?
        Virus.
          Virus who?
        Virus you always singing stupid songs?
            Knock-Knock.
              Who's there?
            Bacilli.
              Bacilli who?
            Don't bacilli!

Knock-Knock.
 Who's there?
Anastasia.
 Anastasia who?
Anastasia out here in the rain.

Knock-Knock.
 Who's there?
Anatol.
 Anatol who?
Anatol you what I thought of you.

Knock-Knock.
 Who's there?
Andalusia.
 Andalusia who?
I'd like to take you someplace Andalusia.

Knock-Knock.
   Who's there?
Andante.
   Andante who?
I'm going to visit my uncle Andante too.

Knock-Knock.
   Who's there?
Andy Green.
   Andy Green who?
"Andy green grass grows all around, all around . . ."

Knock-Knock.
   Who's there?
Anna Maria Alberghetti.
   Anna Maria Alberghetti who?
"Anna Maria Alberghetti in a taxi, honey . . ."

Knock-Knock.
  Who's there?
Annie.
  Annie who?
Annie-body alive in there?

Dracula: Knock-Knock.
  Victim: Who's there?
Dracula: A-One.
  Victim: A-One, who?
Dracula: A-One to drink your blood.

Knock-Knock.
  Who's there?
Apollo.
  Apollo who?
Any Apollo yours is Apollo mine.

Knock-Knock.
  Who's there?
Archer.
  Archer who?
Archer glad to see me?

Knock-Knock.
  Who's there?
Armada.
  Armada who?
Armada told us there'd be days like this.

Knock-Knock.
  Who's there?
Armand.
  Armand who?
Armand the outside looking inside.

Knock-Knock.
    Who's there?
Arne.
    Arne who?
Arne you going to ask me in?

Knock-Knock.
    Who's there?
Arno.
    Arno who?
Arno kids to play with so I'm bored.

Knock-Knock.
    Who's there?
Aruba.
    Aruba who?
Aruba your back, you rub'a mine.

Knock-Knock.
    Who's there?
Ashur.
    Ashur who?
Ashur wish you'd open this door.

        Knock-Knock.
            Who's there?
        Asthma.
            Asthma who?
        Asthma no questions.
                Knock-Knock.
                    Who's there?
                Attila.
                    Attila who?
                Attila no lies.

Knock-Knock.
  Who's there?
Atwood.
  Atwood who?
Atwood be nice if you asked me in.

Knock-Knock.
  Who's there?
Ava.
  Ava who?
Ava seen you someplace before?

Knock-Knock.
  Who's there?
Avenue.
  Avenue who?
Avenue been missing me?

Knock-Knock.
  Who's there?
Avis.
  Avis who?
Avis just at the zoo and thought about you.

Knock-Knock.
  Who's there?
Avocado.
  Avocado who?
Avocado cold. Thad's why I dalk dis way.

Knock-Knock.
  Who's there?
Avon.
  Avon who?
Avon to be alone.

B

Knock-Knock.
  Who's there?
Babylon.
  Babylon who?
Babylon—I'm not listening anyway.

Knock-Knock.
  Who's there?
Banana.
  Banana who?
Banana messages for me?

Knock-Knock.
  Who's there?
Barbie.
  Barbie who?
Barbie Q. Chicken.

Knock-Knock.
  Who's there?
B.C.
  B.C. who?
B.C'ing you!

Knock-Knock.
  Who's there?
Beecher.
  Beecher who?
Beecher at any game you pick.

Knock-Knock.
  Who's there?
Belladonna.
  Belladonna who?
Belladonna work, so I had to knock.

Knock-Knock.
  Who's there?
Belle Lee.
  Belle Lee who?
Belle Lee Dancer.

Knock-Knock.
  Who's there?
Ben and Anna.
  Ben and Anna who?
Ben and Anna split so ice creamed.

Knock-Knock.
  Who's there?
Benny.
  Benny who?
Benny long time no see.

Knock-Knock.
  Who's there?
Beth.
  Beth who?
Beth wisheth, thweetie.

Knock-Knock.
  Who's there?
Blubber.
  Blubber who?
"Blubber, come back to me . . ."

Knock-Knock.
  Who's there?
Bob Dwyer.
  Bob Dwyer who?
Bob Dwyer out here. Caught my pants on it.
  Knock-Knock.
    Who's there?
  Apache.
    Apache who?
  Apache them for you.

Knock-Knock.
  Who's there?
Boise.
  Boise who?
Boise strange!
  Knock-Knock.
    Who's there?
  Idaho.
    Idaho who?
  Idaho. I've seen stranger.

Knock-Knock.
　Who's there?
Boll weevil.
　Boll weevil who?
After the boll weevil all go home.

Knock-Knock.
　Who's there?
Brighton.
　Brighton who?
Up Brighton early just to see you.

Knock-Knock.
　Who's there?
Britches.
　Britches who?
"London Britches falling down . . ."

Knock-Knock.
  Who's there?
Buck.
  Buck who?
"Buck, buck!" I'm a chicken.
    Knock-Knock.
      Who's there?
    Adelaide.
      Adelaide who?
    Adelaide an egg.
        Knock-Knock.
          Who's there?
        Eggs.
          Eggs who?
        Eggs-tremely cold out here in the
        chicken house.

Knock-Knock.
  Who's there?
Budapest.
  Budapest who?
You're nothing Budapest.

C

Knock-Knock.
  Who's there?
Caesar.
  Caesar who?
"Caesar jolly good fellow . . ."

Knock-Knock.
  Who's there?
Cain and Abel.
  Cain and Abel who?
Cain talk now—Abel tomorrow.

Knock-Knock.
  Who's there?
Calder.
  Calder who?
Calder police—I've been robbed!

Knock-Knock.
  Who's there?
Candice.
  Candice who?
Candice be love?

Knock-Knock.
  Who's there?
Cannibal.
  Cannibal who?
Cannibal-eve you're for real!

Knock-Knock.
   Who's there?
Canoe.
   Canoe who?
Canoe please get off my foot?

Knock-Knock.
   Who's there?
Carew.
   Carew who?
The Carew of the Love Boat.

Knock-Knock.
   Who's there?
Caribbean.
   Caribbean who?
You don't Caribbean that I'm standing out here in a snowstorm.

Knock-Knock.
　Who's there?
Carina.
　Carina who?
Carina ditch. Can I use your phone?

Knock-Knock.
　Who's there?
Carmen or Cohen.
　Carmen or Cohen who?
You don't know whether you're Carmen or Cohen.

Knock-Knock.
　Who's there?
Carmencita.
　Carmencita who?
Carmencita down and take a load off your feet.

Knock-Knock.
  Who's there?
Carrie.
  Carrie who?
Carrie me inside—I'm tired.

        Knock-Knock.
          Who's there?
        Cashew.
          Cashew who?
        Cashew see it's me?

Knock-Knock.
  Who's there?
Cecilius.
  Cecilius who?
Cecilius knock-knock joke I ever heard.

Knock-Knock.
  Who's there?
Celeste.
  Celeste who?
Celeste time I saw a face like yours, I threw it a fish.

Knock-Knock.
  Who's there?
Celia.
  Celia who?
Celia later, alligator!

Knock-Knock.
  Who's there?
Charlotta.
  Charlotta who?
Charlotta fuss about nothing.

Knock-Knock.
Who's there?
Cher.
Cher who?
Cher-lock Holmes.

Knock-Knock.
Who's there?
Chesapeake.
Chesapeake who?
Chesapeake to me and I'll tell you everything.

Knock-Knock.
Who's there?
Chess game.
Chess game who?
Chess game to say goodbye.

Knock-Knock.
Who's there?
Chihuahua (pronounced Chi-*wah*-wah).
Chihuahua who?
Chihuahua buy a magazine subscription?

Knock-Knock.
Who's there?
Cinnamon.
Cinnamon who?
Cinnamon-ster—shut the door!

Knock-Knock.
Who's there?
Colin.
Colin who?
Colin the doctor! You make me sick.

Knock-Knock.
Who's there?
Collie.
Collie who?
Collie a taxi. I'm leaving.

Knock-Knock.
Who's there?
Cologne.
Cologne who?
Cologne Ranger!

Knock-Knock.
Who's there?
Comma.
Comma who?
"Comma up and see me sometime."

Knock-Knock.
Who's there?
Concha.
Concha who?
Concha hear me knocking?

Knock-Knock.
  Who's there?
Costanza.
  Costanza who?
Costanza out here in the rain. Open up!

Knock-Knock.
  Who's there?
Cosmo.
  Cosmo who?
You Cosmo trouble than anybody I know.

Knock-Knock.
  Who's there?
Cy.
  Cy who?
Cy knew it was you, I wouldn't have bothered
knocking.

Knock-Knock.
  Who's there?
Czar.
  Czar who?
Czar a doctor in the house?

D

Knock-Knock.
  Who's there?
D-1.
  D-1 who?
  I'm D-1 to watch.

Knock-Knock.
  Who's there?
Dandelion.
  Dandelion who?
Dandelion around
out here, but open the door anyway.

Knock-Knock.
  Who's there?
Danielle.
  Danielle who?
Danielle at me, I heard you the first time.

Knock-Knock.
  Who's there?
Darby.
  Darby who?
Darby a lot of reasons why I knocked.

Knock-Knock.
Who's there?
Darth Vader.
Darth Vader who?
Darth Vader cookie crumbles.

Knock-Knock.
Who's there?
Data.
Data who?
Data new hairdo or did you just walk through a car wash?

Knock-Knock.
    Who's there?
Daughter.
    Daughter who?
Daughter-door salesman!

Knock-Knock.
    Who's there?
Deanna.
    Deanna who?
"Till Deanna time . . ."

Knock-Knock.
    Who's there?
Deluxe.
    Deluxe who?
Deluxe Ness Monster.

Knock-Knock.
    Who's there?
Demand.
    Demand who?
Demand from U.N.C.L.E.

Knock-Knock.
  Who's there?
Dennison.
    Dennison who?
Dennison nice thing to say!

Knock-Knock.
  Who's there?
Derision.
  Derision who?
Derision room for both of us in this town.

Knock-Knock.
  Who's there?
Desi.
  Desi who?
Desi good reason why you think the world is against
you—it is.

Knock-Knock.
  Who's there?
Deuce.
  Deuce who?
Deuce
something
about your
dog. He just
bit me!

Knock-Knock.
　Who's there?
Dexter.
　Dexter who?
"Dexter halls with boughs of holly . . ."

Knock-Knock.
　Who's there?
Diego.
　Diego who?
Diego all over your face—what a sloppy eater!

Knock-Knock.
　Who's there?
Diesel.
　Diesel who?
"Diesel man, he played one, he played nick-nack on a drum . . ."

Knock-Knock.
　Who's there?
Dion.
　Dion who?
Dion of thirst—
can I have a
glass of water?

Knock-Knock.
　Who's there?
Disease.
　Disease who?
Disease a disaster!

Knock-Knock.
Who's there?
Dishes.
Dishes who?
Dishes the police—open the door!

Knock-Knock.
Who's there?
Dishwasher.
Dishwasher who?
Dishwasher last chance.

Knock-Knock.
Who's there?
Dizzy.
Dizzy who?
Dizzy undertaker know you're up?

Knock-Knock.
Who's there?
Doberman pinscher.
Doberman pinscher who?
Doberman pinscher and she slugged him.

Knock-Knock.
Who's there?
Dodson.
Dodson who?
Dodson old Knock-Knock joke.

Knock-Knock.
Who's there?
Domino.
Domino who?
"Domino thing if you don't have that swing . . ."

Knock-Knock.
Who's there?
Don.
Don who?
Don mess around—just open the door.

Knock-Knock.
Who's there?
Donahue.
Donahue who?
Donahue hide from me, you rat.

Knock-Knock.
Who's there?
Donatello.
Donatello who?
Donatello anybody, but I'm a werewolf.

Knock-Knock.
Who's there?
Don Juan.
Don Juan who?
Don Juan to go out today?

Knock-Knock.
　Who's there?
Donat.
　Donat who?
Donat be so smart. Remember, you can always be
replaced by a human being.

Knock-Knock.
　Who's there?
Donovan.
　Donovan who?
Donovan to hear another word out of you.

Knock-Knock.
　Who's there?
Dora Belle.
　Dora Belle who?
Dora Belle is broken. So I knocked.

Knock-Knock.
　Who's there?
Dragon.
　Dragon who?
Dragon my name through the mud?

Knock-Knock.
　Who's there?
Dresden.
　Dresden who?
Dresden rags again?

Knock-Knock.
　Who's there?
Duet.
　Duet who?
Duet right or
don't do it at all.

Knock-Knock.
　Who's there?
Dunbar.
　Dunbar who?
Dunbar the door—I'll only climb through the
window.

Knock-Knock.
　Who's there?
Dutch.
　Dutch who?
Dutch me and I'll scream.

E

Knock-Knock.
  Who's there?
Easter.
  Easter who?
Easter anybody home?

Knock-Knock.
  Who's there?
Eaton.
  Eaton who?
Eaton out of the garbage again?

Knock-Knock.
  Who's there?
Edward B.
  Edward B. who?
Edward B. nice if you made like a bee and buzzed
off.

       Knock-Knock.
        Who's there?
       Efficient.
        Efficient who?
       Efficient my old pal!

Knock-Knock.
　Who's there?
Effie.
　Effie who?
Effie-thing I have is yours.

　　　Knock-Knock.
　　　　Who's there?
　　　Eiffel.
　　　　Eiffel who?
　　　Eiffel down and hurt my knee.
　　　　　Knock-Knock.
　　　　　　Who's there?
　　　　　Antony.
　　　　　　Antony who?
　　　　　Antony still hurts.

Knock-Knock.
  Who's there?
Eileen Dunn
  Eileen Dunn who?
Eileen Dunn the bell and it broke.

Knock-Knock.
  Who's there?
Eisenhower.
  Eisenhower who?
Eisenhower late—sorry!

Knock-Knock.
  Who's there?
Elia.
  Elia who?
Elia wake at night thinking about you.

Knock-Knock.
Who's there?
Emanuel.
Emanuel who?
Emanuel see turn into a werewolf when the moon is full.

Knock-Knock.
Who's there?
Emerson.
Emerson who?
Emerson of a gun!

Knock-Knock.
Who's there?
Emissary.
Emissary who?
Emissary I made you cry.

Knock-Knock.
Who's there?
Eskimo.
Eskimo who?
Eskimo questions—I'll tell you no lies.

Knock-Knock.
Who's there?
Ethan.
Ethan who?
Ethan this the pits?

Knock-Knock.
Who's there?
Eubie.
Eubie who?
Eubie-lieve in law and order—if you lay down the law and give the order.

Knock-Knock.
  Who's there?
Eureka.
    Eureka who?
Eureka perfume! Who sold it to you—a skunk?

Knock-Knock.
  Who's there?
European.
    European who?
European in the neck.

Knock-Knock.
  Who's there?
Evan.
    Evan who?
Evan seen anything like you since the Rocky Horror
Show.

Knock-Knock.
  Who's there?
Eyes.
  Eyes who?
Eyes got another Knock-Knock joke.
    Knock-Knock.
      Who's there?
    Nose.
      Nose who?
    I nose another Knock-Knock joke.
        Knock-Knock.
          Who's there?
        Ears.
          Ears who?
        Ears another Knock-Knock joke.
            Knock-Knock.
              Who's there?
            Chin.
              Chin who?
            Chin up—I'm not going to tell any
            more Knock-Knock jokes.

F

Knock-Knock.
 Who's there?
F-2.
 F-2 who?
Do I F-2 tell you?

Knock-Knock.
 Who's there?
Fanny.
 Fanny who?
Fanny body calls, I'm out.

Knock-Knock.
 Who's there?
Faraday.
 Faraday who?
Faraday last time,
open up!

Knock-Knock.
 Who's there?
Farrah.
 Farrah who?
Farrah out, man.

Knock-Knock.
 Who's there?
Farris.
 Farris who?
"Mirror, mirror on the wall. Who's the Farris
one of all?"

Knock-Knock.
Who's there?
Fedora.
Fedora who?
Fedora shut, does that mean I can't come in?

Knock-Knock.
Who's there?
Ferris.
Ferris who?
Ferris I'm concerned, we're through.

Knock-Knock.
Who's there?
Fess.
Fess who?
Fess Aid Squad.

Knock-Knock.
Who's there?
Fidel.
Fidel who?
Fidel you a secret, will you keep it to yourself?

Knock-Knock.
Who's there?
Fido.
Fido who?
Fido away, what will you give me?

Knock-Knock.
Who's there?
Formosa.
Formosa who?
Formosa the day I've had my foot stuck in this door.

Knock-Knock.
Who's there?
Forty.
Forty who?
Forty last time, open up!

Knock-Knock.
Who's there?
Frank.
Frank who?
Frank N. Stein. Aaggh!

Knock-Knock.
Who's there?
Frank Lee.
Frank Lee who?
Frank Lee, it's none of your business.

Knock-Knock.
Who's there?
Frank's eye.
Frank's eye who?
Frank's eye needed that.

Knock-Knock.
Who's there?
Franz.
Franz who?
Franz forever!

Knock-Knock.
　Who's there?
Fred O.
　Fred O. who?
"Who's a Fred O. the Big Bad Wolf . . ."

Knock-Knock.
　Who's there?
Freedom.
　Freedom who?
Never mind—let freedom ring.

Knock-Knock.
　Who's there?
Free Stew.
　Free Stew who?
The Free Stew-ges (The Three Stooges).

Knock-Knock.
　Who's there?
Freud.
　Freud who?
A-Freud you were going to ask that.

Knock-Knock.
　Who's there?
Fu Manchu.
　Fu Manchu who?
Fu Manchu bubble gum the way you do.

G

Knock-Knock.
  Who's there?
Ghana.
  Ghana who?
Not Ghana take this anymore.

Knock-Knock.
  Who's there?
Alma Gibbons.
  Alma Gibbons who?
Alma Gibbons you 24 hours to get out of town.

Knock-Knock.
  Who's there?
Gideon.
  Gideon who?
Gideon your horse and let's go!

Knock-Knock.
  Who's there?
Gillette.
  Gillette who?
If Gillette me in, I won't knock anymore.

Knock-Knock.
Who's there?
Giovanni.
Giovanni who?
Giovanni come out and play?
Knock-Knock.
Who's there?
Festival.
Festival who?
Festival I have to do my homework.

Knock-Knock.
Who's there?
Gladwin.
Gladwin who?
Gladwin you leave town.

Knock-Knock.
Who's there?
Goat.
Goat who?
Goat to your room!

Knock-Knock.
    Who's there?
Goliath.
    Goliath who?
Goliath down. You're sick in the head.

Knock-Knock.
    Who's there?
Gunboat.
    Gunboat who?
You're Gunboat not forgotten.

Knock-Knock.
    Who's there?
Gunnar.
    Gunnar who?
Gunnar huff and puff and blow your house in.

Knock-Knock.
    Who's there?
Gus.
    Gus who?
That's what *you're*
supposed to do.

Knock-Knock.
    Who's there?
Gucci.
    Gucci who?
Gucci-Gucci-Goo!

52

H

Knock-Knock.
Who's there?
Hackett.
Hackett who?
I can't Hackett—I'm going home.

Knock-Knock.
Who's there?
Haiku.
Haiku who?
"Haiku-d have danced all night . . ."

Knock-Knock.
Who's there?
Halibut.
Halibut who?
Halibut lending me five dollars?

Knock-Knock.
Who's there?
Hallways.
Hallways who?
Hallways knew you'd never amount to much.

Customer: Knock-Knock.
  Waiter: Who's there?
Customer: Hammond.
  Waiter: Hammond who?
Customer: Hammond eggs, please.

Knock-Knock.
  Who's there?
Hans.
  Hans who?
Hans up! I'm a burglar.
  Knock-Knock.
    Who's there?
  Jimmy.
    Jimmy who?
  Jimmy your money—or else!
    Knock-Knock.
      Who's there?
    Bruce.
      Bruce who?
    Careful—I Bruce easily.

Knock-Knock.
  Who's there?
Harley.
  Harley who?
Harley ever see you around anymore.

Knock-Knock.
  Who's there?
Harmony.
  Harmony who?
Harmony times do I have to knock at this door?

Knock-Knock.
  Who's there?
Harris.
  Harris who?
Harris the world treating you?

Knock-Knock.
  Who's there?
Harvard.
  Harvard who?
Harvard you like a punch in the nose?

Knock-Knock.
  Who's there?
Harvey.
  Harvey who?
Harvey going to play this game forever?

Knock-Knock.
  Who's there?
Hattie.
  Hattie who?
Hattie do, you all!

Knock-Knock.
　Who's there?
Heath.
　Heath who?
"For Heath a jolly good fellow . . ."

Knock-Knock.
　Who's there?
Hedda.
　Hedda who?
Hedda feeling you wouldn't open the door.

Knock-Knock.
　Who's there?
Henny.
　Henny who?
Henny Penny. The sky is falling down!
　　Knock-Knock.
　　　Who's there?
　　Izzy.
　　　Izzy who?
　　Izzy end of the world!

Knock-Knock.
　Who's there?
Henrietta.
　Henrietta who?
Henrietta big dinner and got sick.
　　Knock-Knock.
　　　Who's there?
　　Romeo and Juliet.
　　　Romeo and Juliet who?
　　Romeo and Juliet the same thing—and died.

Knock-Knock.
Who's there?
Hester.
Hester who?
Hester any food left?
Knock-Knock.
Who's there?
Pasadena.
Pasadena who?
Pasadena under the door—I'm
starved.

Knock-Knock.
Who's there?
Hewlett.
Hewlett who?
Hewlett you out of your cage?

Knock-Knock.
Who's there?
Hertz.
Hertz who?
Hertz me more than it hurts you.

Knock-Knock.
Who's there?
Heywood, Hugh and Harry.
Heywood, Hugh and Harry who?
Heywood, Hugh Harry and open the door!

Knock-Knock.
Who's there?
Highway cop.
Highway cop who?
Highway cop screaming—thinking of you.

Knock-Knock.
Who's there?
Hobbit.
Hobbit who?
Hobbit letting me in?

Knock-Knock.
  Who's there?
Holden.
  Holden who?
Holden up everything on account of you.

Knock-Knock.
  Who's there?
Holmes.
  Holmes who?
Holmes sweet home.

Knock-Knock.
  Who's there?
Hominy.
  Hominy who?
Hominy rocks did they have to turn up before you crawled out?

Knock-Knock.
   Who's there?
Honda.
   Honda who?
"Home, home Honda range . . ."

Knock-Knock.
   Who's there?
Honeydew.
   Honeydew who?
Honeydew you think you're ever going to open the door?

Knock-Knock.
   Who's there?
Horace.
   Horace who?
Horace I to know you lived here?

Knock-Knock.
   Who's there?
Howard.
   Howard who?
Howard I know?

Knock-Knock.
   Who's there?
Howell.
   Howell who?
Howell I get in if you don't answer the door?

Knock-Knock.
   Who's there?
Hugh Hefner.
   Hugh Hefner who?
Hugh Hefner trouble with the doorknob again?

Knock-Knock.
  Who's there?
Humus.
  Humus who?
Humus be sick—that can't be your real face!

Tap-tap.
  Who's there?
Hurd.
  Hurd who?
Hurd my hand so I can't knock-knock.

Knock-Knock.
  Who's there?
Huron.
  Huron who?
Huron away from home again?

Knock-Knock.
  Who's there?
Hutch.
  Hutch who?
Gesundheit!

Knock-Knock.
  Who's there?
Hy.
  Hy who?
Hy-oh, Silver!

I

Knock-Knock.
  Who's there?
I-one.
  I-one who?
"I-one-der who's kissing her now . . ."

Knock-Knock.
  Who's there?
I.B. Long.
  I.B. Long who?
I.B. Long inside.
It's cold out here.

Knock-Knock.
  Who's there?
Ida.
  Ida who?
Ida know. Sorry.

Knock-Knock.
  Who's there?
Igor.
  Igor who?
Igor to see you again.

Knock-Knock.
Who's there?
Indochina.
Indochina who?
The bull Indochina shop.

Knock-Knock.
Who's there?
Iona.
Iona who?
"Iona have eyes for you . . ."

Knock-Knock.
Who's there?
Ira.
Ira who?
Ira-turn with another Knock-Knock joke.

Knock-Knock.
  Who's there?
Iraq and Iran.
  Iraq and Iran who?
Iraq'd up the car and Iran all the way over.

Knock-Knock.
  Who's there?
Irish Stew.
  Irish Stew who?
Irish Stew would come out and play.

Knock-Knock.
  Who's there?
Isthmus.
  Isthmus who?
Isthmus be the right place.

Knock-Knock.
  Who's there?
Ivan.
  Ivan who?
Ivan infectious disease. (*Slam!*)

Knock-Knock.
  Who's there?
Ivy Leaf.
  Ivy Leaf who?
Ivy Leaf you alone.

J

Knock-Knock.
  Who's there?
Jason.
  Jason who?
"I'm always Jason rainbows . . ."

Knock-Knock.
  Who's there?
Java.
  Java who?
Java lot to learn!

Knock-Knock.
  Who's there?
Jenny.
  Jenny who?
Jenny'd any help opening the door?

Knock-Knock.   Knock-Knock.
  Who's there?   Who's there?
Jess.   Jess me.
  Jess who?   Jess me who?
Jess knock it off!   "Jess me and my shadow . . ."

Knock-Knock.
  Who's there?
Jezebel.
  Jezebel who?
Jezebel on the door, but it won't ring.

Knock-Knock.
  Who's there?
Joe King.
  Joe King who?
You must be Joe King!

Knock-Knock.
  Who's there?
Johannes Sebastian Bach.
  Johannes Sebastian Bach who?
Johannes Sebastian Bach in town!

Knock-Knock.
  Who's there?
John Q.
  John Q. who?
John Q. very much.

Knock-Knock.
  Who's there?
Juana.
  Juana who?
Juana improve your looks? Wear a mask.

Knock-Knock.
Who's there?
Juarez.
Juarez who?
Juarez you hiding, you rascal you?

Knock-Knock.
Who's there?
Judah.
Judah who?
Judah known by now if you opened the door.

Knock-Knock.
Who's there?
Juicy Watt.
Juicy Watt who?
Juicy Watt someone wrote on your door?

Knock-Knock.
  Who's there?
Juneau.
  Juneau who?
Juneau what time it is?
  Knock-Knock.
    Who's there?
  Nome.
    Nome who?
  Nome, I don't.
    Knock-Knock.
      Who's there?
    Alaska.
      Alaska who?
    Alaska someone else.

Knock-Knock.
  Who's there?
Jupiter.
  Jupiter who?
Jupiter hurry or you'll miss the garbage truck.

Knock-Knock.   Knock-Knock.
  Who's there?   Who's there?
Justin.   Justine.
  Justin who?   Justine who?
Justin time for dinner. Justine old-fashioned girl.

        Knock-Knock.
          Who's there?
        Justis.
          Justis who?
        Justis I thought. Wrong door.

K

Knock-Knock.
 Who's there?
Keefe.
 Keefe who?
Keefe me one more chance!

Knock-Knock.
 Who's there?
Keith.
 Keith who?
Keith me, you fool!

Knock-Knock.
 Who's there?
Ken.
 Ken who?
Ken I come in? It's freezing out here.

Knock-Knock.
   Who's there?
Kenya.
   Kenya who?
Kenya keep it down in there?

Knock-Knock.
   Who's there?
Ketchup.
   Ketchup who?
Ketchup with me and I'll tell you.

Knock-Knock.
   Who's there?
Kimona.
   Kimona who?
Kimona my house.

Knock-Knock.
Who's there?
King Kong.
King Kong who?
"King Kong, the witch is dead . . ."

Knock-Knock.
Who's there?
Kip.
Kip who?
Kip talking. Maybe you'll find something to say.

Knock-Knock.
Who's there?
Kojak.
Kojak who?
Kojak up the car. We've got a flat.

Knock-Knock.
Who's there?
Krakatoa.
Krakatoa who?
Just Krakatoa trying to kick this door down!

Knock-Knock.
Who's there?
Kumquat.
Kumquat who?
Kumquat may, we'll always be buddies.

L

Knock-Knock.
  Who's there?
Lava.
  Lava who?
"Lava, come back to me . . ."

Knock-Knock.
  Who's there?
Lemuel.
  Lemuel who?
Lemuel kicked me.
    Knock-Knock.
      Who's there?
    Thor.
      Thor who?
    Thor all over.

Knock-Knock.
  Who's there?
Lee King.
  Lee King who?
Lee King bucket.

Knock-Knock.
  Who's there?
Leonie.
  Leonie who?
Leonie thing you do fast is get tired.

Knock-Knock.
    Who's there?
Lester.
    Lester who?
Lester the Red Hot Mamas.

Knock-Knock.
    Who's there?
Lettuce.
    Lettuce who?
Lettuce in and we'll tell you another Knock-Knock
joke.

Knock-Knock.
    Who's there?
Lion.
    Lion who?
Lion here on your doorstep
till you open the door.

Knock-Knock.
   Who's there?
Lotto.
   Lotto who?
Lotto trouble coming your way if you don't open up.

Knock-Knock.
   Who's there?
Lucas Tell.
   Lucas Tell who?
Lucas Tell-oh and Bud Abbott.

Knock-Knock.
   Who's there?
Lucinda.
   Lucinda who?
Lucinda chain and let me inside.

Knock-Knock.
  Who's there?
Lufthansa.
  Lufthansa who?
Lufthansa! This is a stick-up!

Knock-Knock.
  Who's there?
Luke.
  Luke who?
Luke through the keyhole and see.

Knock-Knock.
  Who's there?
Lyle.
  Lyle who?
Lyle be a monkey's uncle!

M

Scratch-Scratch.
  Who's there?
M-2.
  M-2 who?
M-2 weak to knock.

Knock-Knock.
  Who's there?
Mamie.
  Mamie who?
The Devil Mamie do it!

Knock-Knock.
  Who's there?
Madison.
  Madison who?
You're Madison hatter!

Knock-Knock.
  Who's there?
Mandy.
  Mandy who?
Mandy lifeboats! The ship is sinking!

Knock-Knock.
  Who's there?
Marmoset.
  Marmoset who?
Marmoset there'd be days like this.

Knock-Knock.
  Who's there?
Mary and Abbey.
  Mary and Abbey who?
Mary Christmas and Abbey New Year!

Knock-Knock.
  Who's there?
Maude.
  Maude who?
Maude as well go home.

Knock-Knock.
  Who's there?
Mavis.
  Mavis who?
Mavis be the last time I knock at your door.

Knock-Knock.
   Who's there?
Maynard.
   Maynard who?
Maynard come around anymore if you don't open up.

Knock-Knock.
   Who's there?
Mayonnaise.
   Mayonnaise who?
"Mayonnaise have seen the glory of the coming of
the Lord . . ."

      Knock-Knock.
         Who's there?
      Megan.
         Megan who?
      Megan a phone call.
         Knock-Knock.
            Who's there?
      Jessamyn.
         Jessamyn who?
      Jessamyn-it please—the lion is busy.
         Knock-Knock.
            Who's there?
      Mustang.
         Mustang who?
      Mustang up now—I'm out of change.

Knock-Knock.
   Who's there?
Megan, Elise and Chicken.
   Megan, Elise and Chicken who?
"He's Megan, Elise and Chicken it twice, gonna find out who's naughty and nice . . ."

Knock-Knock.
   Who's there?
Melissa.
   Melissa who?
Melissa to you and I get in trouble.

Knock-Knock.
   Who's there?
Meyer.
   Meyer who?
Meyer in a nasty mood!

Knock-Knock.
  Who's there?
Michael Rhoda.
  Michael Rhoda who?
"Michael Rhoda boat ashore, hallelujah . . ."

Knock-Knock.
  Who's there?
Mike Howe.
  Mike Howe who?
Mike Howe is sick.
    Knock-Knock.
      Who's there?
    Yvette.
      Yvette who?
    Yvette fixed her up.

Knock-Knock.
Who's there?
Mimi.
Mimi who?
Mimi at the pool. I'd like to give you drowning
lessons.

Knock-Knock.
Who's there?
Mindy.
Mindy who?
Mindy mood for pizza.

Knock-Knock.
Who's there?
Nova.
Nova who?
Nova good place for pizza?
Knock-Knock.
Who's there?
Noah.
Noah who?
Noah don't.
Knock-Knock.
Who's there?
Newton.
Newton who?
Newton Monday, but I forgot.

Knock-Knock.
Who's there?
Minna.
Minna who?
Minna wrong place at the wrong time.

Knock-Knock.
Who's there?
Mohair.
Mohair who?
Any Mohair on your head and you could pass for a mop.

Knock-Knock.
Who's there?
Morey and Les.
Morey and Les who?
The Morey I think of you, the Les I think of you.

Knock-Knock.
Who's there?
Mr. T.
Mr. T who?
"Ah, sweet
Mr. T of life . . ."

Knock-Knock.
  Who's there?
Mrs. S. Goode.
    Mrs. S. Goode who?
A Mrs. S. Goode as a mile.

Knock-Knock.
  Who's there?
Murray Lee.
  Murray Lee who?
"Murray Lee we roll along . . ."

Knock-Knock.
  Who's there?
Musket.
  Musket who?
Musket in! The Martians
are after me!

Knock-Knock.
  Who's there?
Mussolini.
  Mussolini who?
Mussolini on your bell
for ten minutes.

Knock-Knock.
  Who's there?
Mustard Bean.
  Mustard Bean who?
You Mustard Bean a big surprise to your parents.
They probably expected a boy or girl.

N

Knock-Knock.
  Who's there?
N.E.
  N.E. who?
N.E. body you like,
as long as
you let me in!

Knock-Knock.
  Who's there?
Needle.
  Needle who?
Needle little attention.

Knock-Knock.
  Who's there?
Nanny.
  Nanny who?
Nanny my friends like you either.

Knock-Knock.
  Who's there?
Nevin.
  Nevin who?
Nevin you mind—just open up.

Knock-Knock.
  Who's there?
Nobel.
  Nobel who?
Nobel, so I knocked.

Knock-Knock.
  Who's there?
Noodle.
  Noodle who?
Never Noodle now where you lived.

Knock-Knock.
  Who's there?
Nutmeg.
  Nutmeg who?
Nutmeg any difference what you say.

O

Knock-Knock.
Who's there?
Odysseus.
Odysseus who?
Odysseus getting boring!

Knock-Knock.
Who's there?
Office.
Office who?
He's Office rocker.

Knock-Knock.
Who's there?
Ohio.
Ohio who?
Ohio feeling?

Knock-Knock.
Who's there?
Olga.
Olga who?
Olga home if you don't treat me better.

Knock-Knock.
Who's there?
Olivia.
Olivia who?
Olivia me alone!

Knock-Knock.
　Who's there?
Ollie or Rex.
　Ollie or Rex who?
Don't put Ollie or Rex in one basket.

Knock-Knock.
　Who's there?
Omaha.
　Omaha who?
Omaha goodness! My hand is caught in the door!

Knock-Knock.
　Who's there?
Omega.
　Omega who?
Omega up your mind.

Knock-Knock.
  Who's there?
Opossum.
  Opossum who?
Opossum by and thought I'd say hello.

Knock-Knock.
  Who's there?
Orangutan.
  Orangutan who?
Orangutan times but you didn't answer.

Knock-Knock.
  Who's there?
Orbach.
  Orbach who?
Front Orbach—you look awful.

Knock-Knock.
Who's there?
Osaka.
Osaka who?
Osaka to me!
Knock-Knock.
Who's there?
Oxford.
Oxford who?
You Oxford it! (*Pow*!)

Knock-Knock.
Who's there?
Oscar and Greta.
Oscar and Greta who?
Oscar foolish question and Greta a foolish answer.

Knock-Knock.
Who's there?
O'Shea.
O'Shea who?
O'Shea it isn't so.

Knock-Knock.
Who's there?
Oslo.
Oslo who?
Oslo on cash. How about a little loan?

Knock-Knock.
   Who's there?
Otto B.
   Otto B. who?
Otto B. a law against people like you.

Knock-Knock.
   Who's there?
Oz.
   Oz who?
Oz out here freezing.

P

Knock-Knock.
  Who's there?
Passion.
  Passion who?
Passion by and thought I'd say hello.

Knock-Knock.
  Who's there?
Pekingese.
  Pekingese who?
Pekingese through the peephole and see.

Knock-Knock.
  Who's there?
Phineas.
  Phineas who?
Phineas thing happened on the way over here . . .

Knock-Knock.
  Who's there?
Preston.
  Preston who?
Preston the doorbell, but it won't ring.

R

Knock-Knock.
  Who's there?
Radio.
  Radio who?
Radio not, here I come!

Knock-Knock.
  Who's there?
Ralph.
  Ralph who?
Ralph! Ralph! I'm a puppy dog!

Knock-Knock.
  Who's there?
Ramona.
  Ramona who?
Ramona going to ask you once more . . .

Knock-Knock.
  Who's there?
Randall.
  Randall who?
Randall the way from the bus.

Knock-Knock.
  Who's there?
Raoul (pronounced Rah-*ool*).
  Raoul who?
"Raoul out the barrel . . ."

Knock-Knock.
  Who's there?
A Raven.
  A Raven who?
A Raven Maniac.

Knock-Knock.
  Who's there?
Rector.
  Rector who?
Rector car. Can I use your phone?

Knock-Knock.
  Who's there?
Reverend.
  Reverend who?
For Reverend ever I've been standing out here . . .

Knock-Knock.
  Who's there?
Rhonda.
  Rhonda who?
Rhonda arrest!

Knock-Knock.
  Who's there?
Ringo.
  Ringo who?
Ringo round the collar.

Knock-Knock.
  Who's there?
Ripon.
  Ripon who?
Ripon up your welcome mat.

Knock-Knock.
  Who's there?
Rollin.
  Rollin who?
"As we come rollin' rollin' home . . ."

Knock-Knock.
Who's there?
Roman.
Roman who?
Roman around with nothing to do.

Knock-Knock.
Who's there?
Rover.
Rover who?
It's all Rover between us.

Knock-Knock.
Who's there?
Rubber Duck.
Rubber Duck who?
"Rubber Duck dub—three men in a tub . . ."

Knock-Knock.
Who's there?
Rumania.
Rumania who?
Can't Rumania out here much longer.

S

Knock-Knock.
  Who's there?
Salem.
  Salem who?
Salem away for good—never have to see you again.

Knock-Knock.
  Who's there?
Sam.
  Sam who?
Sam old story. Ho-hum.

Knock-Knock.
  Who's there?
Samovar.
  Samovar who?
Samovar time you can be a real pest.

Knock-Knock.
  Who's there?
Sancho.
  Sancho who?
Sancho a letter, but you never answered.

96

Knock-Knock.
  Who's there?
Sanctuary.
  Sanctuary who?
Sanctuary much.

Knock-Knock.
  Who's there?
Santa Ana.
  Santa Ana who?
Santa Ana coming to your house because you've
been bad.

Knock-Knock.
  Who's there?
Sarong and Sari.
  Sarong and Sari who?
Sarong house. Sari.

Knock-Knock.
  Who's there?
Satellite.
  Satellite who?
Satellite in the window—one if by land, two if by sea.

Knock-Knock.
   Who's there?
Satin.
   Satin who?
Who Satin my chair?

Knock-Knock.
   Who's there?
Salada.
   Salada who?
Salada bad Knock-Knock jokes around.

Knock-Knock.
Who's there?
Schick.
Schick who?
I'm Schick as a dog.
Knock-Knock.
Who's there?
Esau.
Esau who?
Esau throat is killing me.
Knock-Knock.
Who's there?
Consuelo.
Consuelo who?
Consuelo a thing.

Knock-Knock.
Who's there?
Gargoyle.
Gargoyle who?
Gargoyle with salt water
and you'll feel better.
Knock-Knock.
Who's there?
Hatch.
Hatch who?
I didn't know you
were sick, too.

Knock-Knock.
   Who's there?
Seashell.
   Seashell who?
"Seashell have music wherever she goes . . ."

Knock-Knock.
   Who's there?
Seiko.
   Seiko who?
"Seiko and ye shall find . . ."

Knock-Knock.
   Who's there?
Seminole.
   Seminole who?
"Seminole cowhand—
from the
Rio Grande . . ."

Knock-Knock.
   Who's there?
Senior.
   Senior who?
Senior through the peephole, so I know you're in there.

Knock-Knock.
  Who's there?
Seth.
  Seth who?
Seth me, that's who.

Knock-Knock.
  Who's there?
Shirley M.
  Shirley M. who?
Shirley M. glad to say goodbye to you.

Knock-Knock.
  Who's there?
Shoe buckle.
  Shoe buckle who?
Shoe buckle up your seat belt?

Knock-Knock.
  Who's there?
Shoes.
  Shoes who?
Shoes me, I must
have knocked
on the
wrong door.

Knock-Knock.
   Who's there?
Siam.
   Siam who?
Siam your old pal.

Knock-Knock.
   Who's there?
Siamese.
   Siamese who?
Siamese-y to please.

Knock-Knock.
   Who's there?
Sid.
   Sid who?
"Sid-down, you're rocking the boat . . ."

Knock-Knock.
   Who's there?
Sigrid.
   Sigrid who?
Sigrid Service—open up!

Knock-Knock.
   Who's there?
Simon.
   Simon who?
"Simon the mood for love . . ."

Knock-Knock.
   Who's there?
Simms.
   Simms who?
Simms like I'm always knocking on doors.

Knock-Knock.
   Who's there?
Sinatra.
   Sinatra who?
Sinatra the cough that carries you off, it's the coffin
they carry you off in.

Knock-Knock.
   Who's there?
Sincerely.
   Sincerely who?
Sincerely this morning I've been listening to Knock-
Knock jokes.

Knock-Knock.
  Who's there?
Sis.
  Sis who?
Sis any way to treat a friend?

Knock-Knock.
  Who's there?
Snow.
  Snow who?
Snow use talking to you.

Knock-Knock.
  Who's there?
Sony and Toshiba.
  Sony and Toshiba who?
Sony me, waiting Toshiba.

Knock-Knock.
  Who's there?
Stan.
  Stan who?
Stan back—I'm knocking the door down.

Knock-Knock.
  Who's there?
Stella.
  Stella who?
Stella no answer at the door.

Knock-Knock.
  Who's there?
Stencil.
  Stencil who?
Stencil—there's a bee on your nose.

Knock-Knock.
   Who's there?
Sue.
   Sue who?
Sue-prise—it's me!

Knock-Knock.
   Who's there?
Sumatra.
   Sumatra who?
What's Sumatra with you?

Knock-Knock.
   Who's there?
Swann.
   Swann who?
"Just Swann of those things . . ."

Knock-Knock.
   Who's there?
Swatter.
   Swatter who?
Swatter you complaining about now?

Knock-Knock.
   Who's there?
Sybil.
   Sybil who?
Sybil War!

Knock-Knock.
   Who's there?
Sycamore.
   Sycamore who?
Sycamore Knock-Knock jokes.

T

Knock-Knock.
Who's there?
Tasmania.
Tasmania who?
Tasmania slip between the cup and the lip.

Knock-Knock.
Who's there?
Taurus.
Taurus who?
Taurus closed on my foot. Ouch!

Knock-Knock.
Who's there?
Tennessee.
Tennessee who?
Tennesse you tonight?

Knock-Knock.
Who's there?
Tamara.
Tamara who?
Tamara would be better.

Knock-Knock.
   Who's there?
Terrify.
   Terrify who?
Terrify tissue?

Knock-Knock.
   Who's there?
Thaddeus.
   Thaddeus who?
Thaddeus the silliest thing
I ever heard.

Knock-Knock.
   Who's there?
Theonie.
   Theonie who?
Theonie trouble with your face is that it shows.

Knock-Knock.
   Who's there?
Theophilus.
   Theophilus who?
Theophilus person I ever met is you.

Knock-Knock.
   Who's there?
Thistle.
   Thistle who?
Thistle be the last time I knock on your door.

Knock-Knock.
   Who's there?
Tick.
   Tick who?
Tick 'em up!

108

Knock-Knock.
Who's there?
Titus.
Titus who?
Titus string around your finger so you won't forget
to open the door.

Knock-Knock.
Who's there?
Toad.
Toad who?
Toad you before, but you forgot.

Knock-Knock.
Who's there?
Tobias.
Tobias who?
Are you going Tobias more Knock-Knock books?

Knock-Knock.
   Who's there?
Toledo.
   Toledo who?
It's easy Toledo horse to water, but you can't make him drink.

Knock-Knock.
   Who's there?
Toodle-oo.
   Toodle-oo who?
"Skip Toodle-oo, my darling . . ."

Knock-Knock.
   Who's there?
Toothache.
   Toothache who?
Toothache the high road and I'll take the low road.

Knock-Knock.
  Who's there?
Topeka.
  Topeka who?
Don't open the door. I like Topeka through keyholes.

Knock-Knock.
  Who's there?
Toronto.
  Toronto who?
Have Toronto the store. Can I get you anything?
    Knock-Knock.
      Who's there?
    Canada.
      Canada who?
    Canada best dog food.

Knock-Knock.
  Who's there?
Topol.
  Topol who?
"On Topol Old Smokey . . ."

Knock-Knock.
  Who's there?
Toulouse.
  Toulouse who?
Want Toulouse ten ugly pounds? Cut off your head.

Knock-Knock.
  Who's there?
Trigger.
  Trigger who?
Trigger treat!

Knock-Knock.
Who's there?
Troy.
Troy who?
Troy as I may, I can't reach the bell.

Knock-Knock.
Who's there?
Trudy.
Trudy who?
Can I come Trudy window? The door is stuck.

Knock-Knock.
Who's there?
Turner.
Turner who?
Turner round. You look better from the back.

Knock-Knock.
Who's there?
Two badgers.
Two badgers who?
Two badgers got a chip on your shoulder.

U

Knock-Knock.
Who's there?
U-Boat.
U-Boat who?
U-Boat me a present?

Knock-Knock.
Who's there?
Udall.
Udall who?
Udall know if you opened the door.

Knock-Knock.
Who's there?
Uganda.
Uganda who?
Uganda never guess.

Knock-Knock.
Who's there?
Unicorn.
Unicorn who?
Unicorn-iest guy I ever met.

Knock-Knock.
　Who's there?
Unity.
　Unity who?
Unity sweater for me?

Knock-Knock.
　Who's there?
Upton.
　Upton who?
Upton no good, as usual.

Knock-Knock.
　Who's there?
Ural.
　Ural who?
Ural washed up, kid!

Knock-Knock.
　Who's there?
Utah-Nevada.
　Utah-Nevada who?
Utah-Nevada guessed if I didn't tell you.

V

Knock-Knock.
  Who's there?
Van Gogh.
  Van Gogh who?
Ready—set—Van Gogh!

Knock-Knock.
  Who's there?
Venice.
  Venice who?
Venice these Knock-Knock jokes going to stop?

Knock-Knock.
  Who's there?
Venus.
  Venus who?
Venus see you, I feel sick.

Knock-Knock.
  Who's there?
Vilma.
  Vilma who?
Vilma frog turn into a prince?

W

Knock-Knock.
   Who's there?
Waco (pronounced WAKE-O) and El Paso.
   Waco and El Paso who?
If I can stay Waco for the test, I think El Paso.

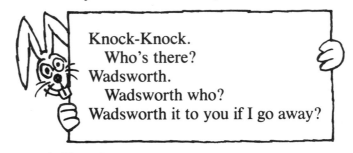

Knock-Knock.
   Who's there?
Wadsworth.
   Wadsworth who?
Wadsworth it to you if I go away?

Knock-Knock.
   Who's there?
Wallaby.
   Wallaby who?
Wallaby in trouble if I keep knocking on the door?

Knock-Knock.
   Who's there?
Wanamaker.
   Wanamaker who?
Wanamaker mud pie?

Knock-Knock.
   Who's there?
Warsaw.
   Warsaw who?
Warsaw Knock-Knock joke I ever heard.

Knock-Knock.
   Who's there?
Watts.
   Watts who?
Watts up, Doc?

Knock-Knock.
   Who's there?
Weasel.
   Weasel who?
"Weasel while you work . . ."

Knock-Knock.
   Who's there?
Wednesday.
   Wednesday who?
"Wednesday saints go marching in . . ."

Knock-Knock.
   Who's there?
Wendy Katz.
   Wendy Katz who?
Wendy Katz away, the mice will play.

Knock-Knock.
   Who's there?
Werner.
   Werner who?
Werner you going to grow up?

Knock-Knock.
Who's there?
Whelan.
Whelan who?
That's all Whelan good, but I still think you're a nut.

Knock-Knock.
Who's there?
Whitmore.
Whitmore who?
Whitmore can I say after I say I'm sorry?

Knock-Knock.
Who's there?
Whittier.
Whittier who?
Whittier think my chances are for getting inside?

Knock-Knock.
Who's there?
Who.
Who who?
Terrible echo in here, isn't there?

Knock-Knock.
Who's there?
Widow.
Widow who?
A Widow Kid.

Knock-Knock.
Who's there?
Wiener.
Wiener who?
Wiener takes all.

Knock-Knock.
Who's there?
Willard.
Willard who?
Willard be too late if I come back in an hour?

Knock-Knock.
   Who's there?
William Tell.
   William Tell who?
William Tell your mommy to come to the door?

Knock-Knock.
   Who's there?
Willoughby.
   Willoughby who?
Willoughby my Valentine?
      Knock-Knock.
         Who's there?
      Willie.
         Willie who?
      Willie or won't he?

Knock-Knock.
  Who's there?
Winnie.
  Winnie who?
Winnie you going to open the door?

Knock-Knock.
  Who's there?
Winott.
  Winott who?
Winott leave your brain to science? Maybe they can find a cure for it.

Knock-Knock.
  Who's there?
Wolf.
  Wolf who?
Wolf-er goodness sake, Grandma, what big teeth you have!

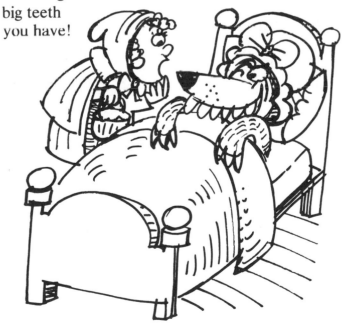

Knock-Knock.
  Who's there?
Woody.
  Woody who?
Woody you care who this is?

Knock-Knock.
  Who's there?
Wyatt.
  Wyatt who?
Wyatt the world do I bother to talk to you?

Knock-Knock.
  Who's there?
Wyden.
  Wyden who?
Wyden you tell me you were a werewolf?

Knock-Knock.
  Who's there?
Wynn.
  Wynn who?
Wynn a few—lose a few.

Y

Knock-Knock.
  Who's there?
Yeti.
  Yeti who?
Yeti-nother Knock-Knock joke!

Knock-Knock.
  Who's there?
Yoko.
  Yoko who?
Yoko jump in the lake.

Knock-Knock.
  Who's there?
Yokum.
  Yokum who?
"Yokum a long way, baby . . ."

Knock-Knock.
  Who's there?
Yucatan.
  Yucatan who?
Yucatan dollars to pay the taxi?

Knock-Knock.
  Who's there?
Yucca.
  Yucca who?
Yucca be arrested for impersonating a human being.

Knock-Knock.
  Who's there?
Yul.
  Yul who?
Yul look wonderful. Who is your embalmer?

Knock-Knock.
  Who's there?
Yule.
  Yule who?
Yule never guess.

Knock-Knock.
  Who's there?
Yuma.
  Yuma who?
The Good Yuma man.

Knock-Knock.
  Who's there?
Yuri
  Yuri who?
Yuri mind me of the
Liberty Bell—
half-cracked.

Z

Knock-Knock.
  Who's there?
Zenka.
  Zenka who?
Zenka you for your kind words.

Knock-Knock.
  Who's there?
Zinc.
  Zinc who?
Zinc of you all the time—turkey!

Knock-Knock.
  Who's there?
Zinnia.
  Zinnia who?
There's method Zinnia madness.

Knock-Knock.
  Who's there?
Zipper and Zipper.
  Zipper and Zipper who?
"Zipper D. Doodah and Zipper D.A. . . ."

Knock-Knock.
 Who's there?
Zuccarelli.
 Zuccarelli who?
Zuccarelli long time to get to the last Knock-Knock
joke.